A GOD

WHO

HIDES

HIMSELF

WITNESS LEE

LIVING STREAM MINISTRY
Anaheim, California • www.lsm.org

ISBN 978-1-57593-983-4

Living Stream Ministry
2431 W. La Palma Ave., Anaheim, CA 92801
P. O. Box 2121, Anaheim, CA 92814 USA

14 15 16 17 / 11 10 9 8 7

A GOD WHO HIDES HIMSELF

Scripture Reading: Isa. 45:15; 1 Kings
19:9-18; Luke 24:13-37; John 20:11-29;
1 Pet. 1:8

Have you ever noticed this statement
in the Bible—"a God who hides Himself"?
I have tested numbers of brothers and
sisters with this question and have made
the discovery that scarcely any of God's
children have realized that His Word
contains such an expression; nor do they
really know God as a God who hides
Himself. They know Him as the almighty
One, as the righteous One, as One full of
grace and compassion; but as the One who
hides Himself, He is unknown to them.

Note how Isaiah expresses this
thought: "Surely You are a God who hides
Himself, O God of Israel." This statement of his is most emphatic. He is not
talking empty words, the fruit of his own
imagination; his utterance is based on an
accumulation of facts. He has looked at

those facts, he has studied those facts, and then he has come to his conclusion: "You are a God who hides Himself, O God." What he has seen of God's doings, what he has observed happen to Israel under the hand of God, what he has beheld of the experiences of God's people—all these observations have forced the prophet to acknowledge that God is a God who hides Himself. Why did Isaiah come to this conclusion? If you read his book through, you will discover. It was because God did countless things in the midst of the children of Israel and countless things in their personal lives, yet He concealed Himself. He was ceaselessly working, yet He was always hidden. Very much was being done by Him, yet the Israelites were utterly ignorant as to who the doer was. Then one day Isaiah exclaimed, "Surely You are a God who hides Himself, O God."

Our personalities are diametrically opposed to God's personality. He likes concealment, we like display; He does not crave outward manifestations, we cannot be content without them. This divine disposition constitutes a great trial and test to us.

"Elijah was a man of like feeling with us," and he did not stand this test. On Mount Carmel God was obviously with him; but when God withheld His manifest presence, Elijah could not bear it. He became depressed and crept into a cave. When God asked him, "What doest thou here?" he answered, "I have been very jealous for the Lord God of hosts: for the children of Israel have forsaken thy covenant, thrown down thine altars, and slain thy prophets with the sword; and I, even I only, am left; and they seek my life, to take it away." God knew Elijah's difficulty; He knew Elijah wanted Him to be a God who would manifest Himself; he had not realized that God is a God who hides Himself. So God gave him a demonstration. There arose "a great and strong wind." Elijah thought: The Lord is in this! "But the Lord was not in the wind." The wind was followed by an earthquake. Elijah thought: Surely the Lord is in this! "But the Lord was not in the earthquake." Then came a fire, and Elijah thought: The Lord

3

is a consuming fire, He'll be in this! "But the Lord was not in the fire." After the fire came a still small voice—and the Lord was in that! Elijah said to Him, "I, even I only, am left"; but the Lord very gently answered, "There are seven thousand persons who have not bowed down to Baal. Elijah, I hide Myself; you did not know I had preserved those seven thousand souls." Elijah had reckoned only with what he could see; but God is a God who hides Himself. He was not in the wind, nor in the earthquake, nor in the fire; He was in the still small voice. He had preserved for Himself seven thousand persons who had not bowed the knee to Baal; but so hidden was His activity, not even the prophet Elijah knew anything about it.

I long that God's children might realize the hidden nature of His working. Do not think that only mighty influences, great visions, and tremendous revelations are of Him. God's surest work is done in the secret of our beings. Often it is just a slight whisper or a slight influence— so slight we can scarcely distinguish it from our own impressions. This is God's mightiest mode of activity. Sometimes from our innermost being comes a faint suggestion (or shall I call it a feeling? or a voice? or words?) saying something like this: "That's your natural life; that belongs to the cross"—saying it in words that are scarcely words; but do please take note, these almost indefinable words are indications of God's most positive activity. You may reason: This is not God; it's just me. But let me assure you, this is His most definite speaking and working. It is such divine activity that has preserved the church throughout her history of nearly two thousand years. The more we serve the Lord, and the more we abide in Him, the more we realize that God is a very quiet God, so quiet that His presence is often undetected. His most intimate way of guiding us is so natural that we scarcely perceive He is guiding us at all, yet somehow we have been led; something has happened. It is often by this quiet, inward activity of God that we receive our greatest guidances.

If you look into the history of the universe, if you look into the history of the

Old Testament and into the history of the New, and if you carefully examine the whole history of mankind, you will arrive at the same conclusion: God is a God who hides Himself. This universe was created by Him; the heavens and the earth are the works of His hand; yet for six millennia men have beheld all these things and not one man has ever seen God. The Scripture says of the Old Testament times that no man ever saw Him; but of the New Testament times it says, "The only begotten Son, who is in the bosom of the Father, He has declared Him" (John 1:18).

And yet, when this only begotten Son came for the very purpose of showing forth the Father, He hid Him in a human life—a human life whose "appearance was marred," a human life that had "no attracting form nor majesty" (Isa. 52:14; 53:2). And He came from Galilee, an insignificant province, and from the town of Nazareth, a small town of which it was said by the Jews that no prophet or person of repute ever came from there (John 1:46; 7:52). So, when He appeared, people not only found it hard to believe that God was present in Him—they found it hard even to believe that He was a prophet of God. Yet God was hidden within Jesus of Nazareth.

One day, as I was pondering this, it occurred to me as an amazing thing that God, who obviously desired to manifest Himself, should have hidden Himself from men for four thousand years—from the creation to the end of the Old Testament period. And when, in the New Testament period, He came from heaven to earth for the special purpose of revealing Himself to men, He hid Himself once more—hid Himself in man. He appears and then hides, and He hides Himself so effectively that no one can possibly recognize Him. It seems as though He likes to act that way. I believe He knows I do not mean it irreverently if I say: That is His temperament!

Let me illustrate. There are some brothers and sisters who, whatever they do, do it most unobtrusively. If they bring you a drink of water, they watch for an opportunity when you are looking out of the window, then steal in quietly, put down the water, and steal out again. When you turn around you see a glass of water but have no idea who put it there. I have met many brothers and sisters who do things like that. When they do anything for you, they do it so silently and secretly, you don't know who has done it. And we say— That's their temperament! But there are brothers and sisters of a totally different disposition. They always make a great display. If they bring you a glass of water, they bang the glass so that the noise reaches you before the water does; then in they walk with a great flourish and say, "A glass of water, Brother So-and-so!"

Once I visited a certain church where one of the sisters had been appointed to act as hostess. Oh! that sister simply filled the place. She was so big she obscured the whole church; I could not catch sight of the elders, or the deacons, or the brothers, or the sisters for the sight of her. Wherever I looked, there she was. If she brought you anything, she always did it ostentatiously. Let me tell you, brothers and sisters, that was her temperament!

Let me tell you, our God is not like that. He never makes any display: He is too great. But the marvel is that He remains so hidden. We know He is great, exceedingly great, unutterably great; yet He could make Himself small enough to take up His abode in a man, Jesus of Nazareth. And this man belonged to a poor home and grew up to be a carpenter— a very ordinary carpenter, working in a very small way, until He was thirty. Whoever would have thought He was indwelt by God, the infinite God? True, after He entered upon His public ministry, He did at times work signs and wonders, and He did at times say extraordinary things; but then He would withdraw and hide Himself again.

If you study the Scriptures carefully, you will see that God has the kind of temperament that dislikes ostentation. He likes to work secretly rather than openly. He created the universe and then hid Himself in it, until we do not know where to find Him. He took up His abode in a man, but that man was almost unknowable. On first meeting Him, men just saw a man called Jesus, of Nazareth. On meeting Him a second time, they recognized in

Him a man of more than average intellect; and on the third time of meeting, they thought He must be a prophet. When they met Him still later, they felt, "Oh, this man is surely more than a prophet!" But to discover exactly who He was, was no easy matter. Even His disciples, during their three and a half years in His company, did not arrive at a true knowledge of Him. All this tells us that He was continually hiding Himself. He would manifest Himself for a moment and then would conceal Himself again.

Once, on the Mount of Transfiguration, He revealed Himself clearly; but He hid again and even told the three who were with Him not to tell others what they had seen. And though they had been witnesses of the transfiguration, later on they themselves were tossed between faith and doubt. What was the cause of their bewilderment? Just this— that no sooner had He revealed Himself than He would hide Himself once more.

Though Christianity has spread all over the world, not a soul can say that his eyes have actually beheld Jesus. It is a startling fact that, though Christianity has such a place on the earth, Jesus is concealed from the earth. Brothers and sisters, does the wonder of it not strike you? Do you believe in the Lord Jesus? You say, "Yes." Do you love the Lord Jesus? You say, "I do." The heathen may ask you, "Where did you meet Him?" And not only will they raise questions, you yourself will raise questions. I remember when, over twenty years ago, I used to wonder if I had been deceived. I loved Jesus intensely, I believed in Him heartily; but I had never seen Him. Had I perhaps come under the influence of men? How could I love someone I had never seen? How could I believe in someone my eyes had never beheld? I began to doubt.

But the astonishing thing was this—just as I was questioning, I fell on my knees and prayed, "O Lord Jesus, You are too good; You are too lovable; You are too trustworthy." And even while I was kneeling in prayer, this mind of mine was still saying, "Perhaps I've been deceived. Where is Jesus? Have you ever seen Him?" But, all the while my mind was

11

questioning, my heart was saying, "O Lord Jesus, how I thank You! You died for me on the cross, and now You are in heaven as my Mediator, and Your Holy Spirit is within me." Just see those two streams of life—the outer man doubting, the inner man praying! Is it not surprising that often both of these experiences are simultaneous?

Now, why have I spent so much time elaborating this one point? So that God's children may see that in all His intercourse with us, in all His activity in our lives, His ways are in keeping with His disposition. Just as we, in our intercourse with our friends, inevitably act in accordance with *our* dispositions, so God, in all His relations with us, is true to *His* disposition. And what is His disposition? It is a disposition that hides itself. He is very active and yet very hidden; He is truly present and yet so concealed that you can be totally unconscious of His presence. If at any time you become aware of Him, He will change His activity and that awareness will go.

Our Lord Jesus had close intercourse

with His disciples for three and a half years. Little by little He made Himself known to them until they began to realize that He was a man indwelt by God. How they appreciated Him then! They looked at Him, they touched Him, and one of them even reclined on His breast. Just as they really thought they possessed Him, however, He broke in with these startling words: "I go away"! They were all deeply distressed. Formerly they had not known Him; now they knew Him, now they appreciated Him, now they prized Him; and now—just as they thought they really had Him forever—He spoke of leaving them. How could He? But listen to what He said: "It is expedient for you that I go away." His disciples were more perplexed than ever. "Expedient for you that I go away"? Yes, "expedient...for if I do not go away, the Comforter will not come to you." Who is He? "He" is still "I." "*I* am going away and *I* am coming to you." "*I* will not leave you as orphans; *I* am coming to you" (John 14:18, 28; 16:5-16).

Did He go away and come again? Yes. But here is the remarkable point. When

He left them, they knew it; when He came again, they were ignorant of it. Is not that astounding? You remember, when He rose from the dead and appeared to men, Mary stood there weeping, and she "beheld Jesus standing there, yet she did not know that it was Jesus." As soon as He called, "Mary," she recognized the Lord and wanted to touch Him. But He said, "Do not touch Me"—and presently He was gone! (John 20:14-17). Do you see? When you are not clear, He comes to you; as soon as you are clear, He goes. That is His disposition! He comes all unseen; as soon as you have seen Him, He has gone.

I love to read Luke 24. I think: What nonsense those two disciples talked on the way to Emmaus! (But I sometimes discover myself to be one of the two!) Just as those sad-faced disciples were walking along the road, mournfully communing with one another about the death of their Lord, suddenly Someone joined them and asked what they were talking about. "What?" they said. "Do you mean to say you've been staying in Jerusalem and don't know what has happened?" How

14

great our Lord is! He simply asked, "What has happened?" And as they walked along, slowly pouring out their long tale of woe, He patiently accompanied them and patiently listened. When they had concluded their tale, He said, "O foolish and slow of heart to believe in all that the prophets have spoken!" Up to this point the two were still unenlightened; but they must have been impressed by the Stranger, for when they reached the village and Jesus "acted as though He would go farther...they constrained Him" to stay with them. And when they invited Him to eat, He quite unceremoniously assumed the place of host, "took the loaf and blessed it, and having broken it, He began handing it to them." At that point "their eyes were opened, and they recognized Him." And here is the amazing thing: When they could not see, He could listen; when they talked nonsense, He could go out of His way and accompany them for a long time; but as soon as their eyes were opened, "He disappeared from them." That is His disposition!

Let me assure you, when you cannot

see the Lord, He is listening to all your foolish talk and is going out of His way to accompany you. I have found myself talking to a brother after this fashion: "These days the Lord is not with us. The meetings are so heavy; those who should open their lips keep them closed. It seems as though the Lord has forsaken us." When I discover myself talking like that, I dare not go on, for I am afraid He will hear me talking nonsense. Brothers and sisters, I long that we might all realize that, since the resurrection of our Lord, the chief discipline for His followers has come along the line of knowing Him as a God who hides Himself. He is in the midst of men, yet does not show Himself to men; He dwells within, yet withholds the consciousness of His indwelling. He is truly in you, and is truly working in you, and working wonderful things, tremendous things; but His disposition is not the disposition of the one we spoke of who loved to make a display. He is a God who hides Himself.

Let me cite another illustration. One evening, when the doors were shut where some of His disciples were gathered, the

Lord appeared. Later Thomas came along and declared, "Unless I see in His hands the mark of the nails and put my finger into the mark of the nails and put my hand into His side, I will by no means believe." The Lord felt for him in his weakness, and one day He allowed him to see and to feel. Then Thomas bowed his head and worshipped, saying, "My Lord and my God." But Jesus said to him, "Because you have seen Me, you have believed. Blessed are those who have not seen and have believed" (John 20:24-29). "Your disposition is one that loves to see, but I love a disposition that believes where it cannot see, for I like to hide Myself."

Peter had some experience by the time he wrote his first Epistle, and he could say, "Whom having not seen, you love." That is a marvelous thing. Where would you find a man who could love a fellow man he had never seen? But Peter says that, though you have never seen the Lord, you love Him; and he goes on to say, "In whom though not seeing Him at present, yet believing, you exult with joy that is unspeakable and full of glory" (1 Pet. 1:8). Faith and love are in an unseen One.

May the Lord show us how different He is from our conception of Him. If there is great exhilaration in our meetings, we say, "Oh, the Lord is truly in the midst!" But such a condition is no evidence of reality. On the other hand, when the atmosphere is heavy and you find yourself thinking thoughts like these:—"Alas! I don't love the Lord as I ought. How reluctant I've been to pay the price! How I've failed to honor Him in my life!"—then the God who hides Himself is positively at work in your life. Sometimes when you are out on the street or in your room, thoughts such as these come to you—"What is the purpose of my life? What is the Lord getting out of it?"—and it does not dawn upon you that that is the Lord at work within you. Let me tell you: Those faint registrations in the depths of your being, those slight suggestions you thought were wholly your own because they were so natural—those were the Lord's doing. The God who hides Himself is at work within your life, but He has hidden Himself so effectively that you have been quite unconscious of His activity. And He is working outwardly as well as inwardly—in your home, in your business, in all your circumstances. He is creating many situations and is active in many directions, though He lets you sense nothing of it, until you imagine these things have just come about naturally; but both the inner and outer conditions of your life are under His control.

The very fact that the church has continued on this earth for nearly two thousand years is the result of the working of Him who is a God who hides Himself. It is often true that the greater the display accompanying any work, the less the divine content; and the more silent the work and the less our awareness of it, the greater the divine content. Since all the work we do is done unto Him who hides Himself, it must be based on faith, not on sight.

I trust these words will help some of us to realize that when we are most conscious of impotence, God is often most powerfully present. Don't look for greater things. Don't look for things other than they are.

Don't set your expectation on some great vision or on some great experience. And don't expect anything outward, for the God who hides Himself is at work within your life, and He is working mightily. Your responsibility is to cooperate with Him by responding to His voice within—that "still small voice," that voice that seems so much a part of your own feelings that you scarcely recognize it as a voice at all. To that voice, registered in the deepest depths of your being, you must say, "Amen," for there, secretly and ceaselessly, the God who hides Himself is working.